YAS

W9-BAU-114

Writing the Critical Essay

GLOBAL WARMING

An OPPOSING VIEWPOINTS® Guide

Mary E. Williams, *Book Editor*

Bonnie Szumski, *Publisher, Series Editor*
Helen Cothran, *Managing Editor*

OPPOSING
VIEWPOINTS®
SERIES

GREENHAVEN PRESS
An imprint of Thomson Gale, a part of The Thomson Corporation

THOMSON
✦
GALE

Detroit • New York • San Francisco • San Diego • New Haven, Conn. • Waterville, Maine • London • Munich

THOMSON

---*---

GALE

LIBRARY OF CONGRESS CATALOGING-IN-PUBLICATION DATA
Global warming / Mary E. Williams, book editor. 　p. cm. — (Writing the critical essay) 　　Includes bibliographical references and index. 　ISBN 0-7377-3210-5 (lib. bdg. : alk. paper) 　1. Global warming. 2. Essay—Authorship. 3. Rhetoric. I. Williams, Mary E., 1960– II. Series. 　QC981.8.G56G5745 2006
2005055066

Printed in the United States of America

CONTENTS

Examining the state of writing and how it is taught in the United States was the official purpose of the National Commission on Writing in America's Schools and Colleges. The commission, made up of teachers, school administrators, business leaders, and college and university presidents, released its first report in 2003. "Despite the best efforts of many educators," commissioners argued, "writing has not received the full attention it deserves." Among the findings of the commission was that most fourth-grade students spent less than three hours a week writing, that three-quarters of high school seniors never receive a writing assignment in their history or social studies classes, and that more than 50 percent of first-year students in college have problems writing error-free papers. The commission called for a "cultural sea change" that would increase the emphasis on writing for both elementary and secondary schools. These conclusions have made some educators realize that writing must be emphasized in the curriculum. As colleges are demanding an ever-higher level of writing proficiency from incoming students, schools must respond by making students more competent writers. In response to these concerns, the SAT, an influential standardized test used for college admissions, required an essay for the first time in 2005.

Books in the Writing the Critical Essay: An Opposing Viewpoints Guide series use the patented Opposing Viewpoints format to help students learn to organize ideas and arguments and to write essays using common critical writing techniques. Each book in the series focuses on a particular type of essay writing—including expository, persuasive, descriptive, and narrative—that students learn while being taught both the five-paragraph essay as well as longer pieces of writing that have an opinionated focus. These guides include everything necessary to help students research, outline, draft, edit, and ultimately write successful essays across the curriculum, including essays for the SAT.

Using Opposing Viewpoints

This series is inspired by and builds upon Greenhaven Press's acclaimed Opposing Viewpoints series. As in the parent series, each book in the Writing the Critical Essay series focuses on a timely and controversial social issue that provides lots of opportunities for creating thought-provoking essays. The first section of each volume begins with a brief introductory essay that provides context for the opposing viewpoints that follow. These articles are chosen for their accessibility and clearly stated views. The thesis of each article is made explicit in the article's title and is accentuated by its pairing with an opposing or alternative view. These essays are both models of persuasive writing techniques and valuable research material that students can mine to write their own informed essays. Guided reading and discussion questions help lead students to key ideas and writing techniques presented in the selections.

The second section of each book begins with a preface discussing the format of the essays and examining characteristics of the featured essay type. Model five-paragraph and longer essays then demonstrate that essay type. The essays are annotated so that key writing elements and techniques are pointed out to the student. Sequential, step-by-step exercises help students construct and refine thesis statements; organize material into outlines; analyze and try out writing techniques; write transitions, introductions, and conclusions; and incorporate quotations and other researched material. Ultimately, students construct their own compositions using the designated essay type.

The third section of each volume provides additional research material and writing prompts to help the student. Additional facts about the topic of the book serve as a convenient source of supporting material for essays. Other features help students go beyond the book for their research. Like other Greenhaven Press books, each book in the Writing the Critical Essay series includes bibliographic listings of relevant periodical articles, books, Web sites, and organizations to contact.

Writing the Critical Essay: An Opposing Viewpoints Guide will help students master essay techniques that can be used in any discipline.

Background to Controversy: The Heated Debate Surrounding Global Warming

E arly in the summer of 1988, temperatures reached a sweltering 101°F (38°C) in Washington, D.C. That day, NASA scientist James Hansen gave some now-famous and disturbing testimony before the U.S. Senate Committee on Energy and Natural Resources. Hansen later discussed the conclusions he had shared with Congress: "The first was that I believed the earth was getting warmer, and I could say that with 99 percent confidence. The second was that with a high degree of confidence we could associate the warming and the greenhouse effect." In addition, he maintained, the "evidence was strong"[1] that human-made pollutants were intensifying the greenhouse effect and thereby raising world temperatures. If temperatures continued to rise, Hansen warned, the planet would face disastrous climate changes that would harm humans and the environment.

The Greenhouse Effect

The greenhouse effect is an essential part of Earth's climate. When energy from the sun reaches the planet, it is absorbed by oceans and land masses. Some of that solar heat is radiated back through the atmosphere, which is made up of many gases. The greenhouse gases, including water vapor, carbon dioxide, and nitrous oxide, absorb this radiated heat, creating a blanket of warm air around Earth. This layer of warmth moderates global temperatures and climate patterns, making Earth into a greenhouse abounding with life. Without the greenhouse effect, Earth would exist in a perpetual ice age.

The Greenhouse Effect

1 The Sun releases energy in the form of light and heat. About 70 percent of the Sun's heat is absorbed by land, air, and the oceans.

2 About 30 percent of the Sun's heat reflects off the Earth's surface and atmosphere back into space.

3 Some of the reflected heat is trapped by greenhouse gases in the Earth's atmosphere. Global warming occurs when high levels of greenhouse gases trap more heat.

The problem occurs when the levels of atmospheric greenhouse gases increase. The connection between humanity, the greenhouse effect, and global warming, many scientists say, started with the Industrial Revolution of the 1700s. At that time fossil fuels began being used in large amounts. The burning of fossil fuels, such as coal, oil, and natural gas, results in higher amounts of greenhouse gases in the atmosphere. In addition, nitrous oxide, found in fertilizer, is released through farming. Coal mining and petroleum drilling emit methane into the atmosphere. And carbon dioxide is a by-product of automobile and power plant emissions. Other human activities, from barbecuing to deforestation, raise the amount of greenhouse gases in the atmosphere. And higher atmospheric concentrations of greenhouse gases, many experts say, create higher global temperatures.

Predictions About Global Warming

Scientific data reveal that the levels of several greenhouse gases have risen dramatically. As environmental researcher Kenneth Green explains, "From the late 1700s to the present, carbon dioxide levels have increased by

A Bangladeshi woman and her children wade through flooded streets in 2004. Some scientists fear global warming will cause a dramatically higher incidence of flooding.

nearly 30 percent. Concentrations of methane, an even stronger warming gas, have increased nearly 150 percent since the beginning of the nineteenth century, while nitrous oxide levels have increased by about 22 percent from the preindustrial era."[2] The result, some climatologists say, is a global temperature increase of 1°F (0.556°C) over the past one hundred years. Some predict an additional increase of 3° to 10°F (1.7° to 5.56°C) over the next one hundred years. Such a temperature change is likely to cause glacial melting, rising sea levels, and a greater incidence of floods, droughts, heat waves, wildfires, hurricanes, and other forms of extreme weather, analysts maintain. These climate changes could in turn lead to an increase in storm-related deaths, infectious diseases, economic disasters, environmental damage, and species extinctions, they warn.

Criticism of the Global Warming Theory

Not all analysts agree that global warming is as serious and far-reaching as many scientists have claimed. Critics often point to certain data inconsistencies. For example, though global warming is allegedly accelerating, there is little evidence that sea levels have risen accordingly. In addition, many of the predictions about global warming are based on computerized models that have proven unreliable. Global temperature readings taken on the ground, from satellites, and from weather balloons often contradict the predictions of the computer models. As astrophysicist Sallie Baliunas points out, no warming of the lower troposphere (the atmosphere between 5,000 and 28,000 feet [1,524 and 8,534m] above the ground) has been recorded, even though forecasts suggested that tropospheric warming should have already occurred because of increased carbon dioxide levels. "No catastrophic human-made global warming effects can be found in the best measurements of climate that we presently have," says Baliunas. "Human-made global

warming is relatively minor and will be slow to develop, affording us an opportunity to continue to improve observations."[3]

World Response to Global Warming

Dozens of world leaders have responded to concerns about global warming by signing the Kyoto Protocol, an agreement among 140 industrialized nations to cut greenhouse-gas emissions by 8 percent by the year 2012. This global climate treaty went into effect in February 2005; however, the United States did not sign this agreement due to concerns about how it would affect the economy. Critics of the treaty argued that it would have been too expensive for U.S. companies and factories to adopt

Japanese activists celebrate the enactment of the Kyoto Protocol, an agreement among dozens of industrialized nations to curb emissions of greenhouse gases.

pollution-reducing technologies. Others claim that the treaty is not very effective because many poor countries will still be allowed to use technologies that produce greenhouse gases.

Global warming obviously remains a point of contention among scientists, environmentalists, politicians, media analysts, and corporate leaders. The viewpoints that follow offer a variety of opinions about this much-discussed issue.

Notes

1. James Hansen, testimony before the U.S. Senate Committee on Energy and Natural Resources, June 23, 1988.

2. Kenneth Green, "Heated Debate over a Hot Theory," *World & I,* January 2001.

3. Sallie Baliunas, "The Kyoto Protocol and Global Warming," *Imprimus,* March 2002.

Section One:
Opposing
Viewpoints
on Global
Warming

Global Warming Causes Extreme Weather

Tim Dickinson

Tim Dickinson writes that global warming has made the planet's weather more extreme. Heat waves, record droughts, melting glaciers, and severe flooding have increased in recent years. All of these prove that climate change is occurring, the author maintains. He cites analysts who agree that these changes are caused by burning fossil fuels. This process releases carbon dioxide and other greenhouse gases that warm up the atmosphere. While it may be too late to stop global warming, the author concludes, it is still possible to slow it down and prevent catastrophe. Dickinson is a writer in San Francisco, California.

Consider the following questions:

1. According to Dickinson, how many Europeans died of heat-related ailments in 2003?
2. How does significant tropical climate change show up in Venezuela and Kenya, according to Dickinson?
3. By how many degrees has the temperature in Alaska increased over the past fifty years, according to the author?

The hospitals and funeral parlors of Paris could not keep up with the dead. As morgues filled to overflowing, delivery trucks were pressed into service and bodies stowed in their refrigerated bays. The city set up inflatable tents, chilled to prevent the corpses from rotting, yet still they came—casualties by the hundreds, then thousands. In desperation, the government requisitioned a former produce market and lined the concrete floor of its cavernous warehouse with 700 army cots, arranged in tight green rows. For many victims, Rue des Glacieres—Refrigerator Street—became their next-to-final resting place.

Extreme Weather

The victims did not perish in a chemical leak, a train bombing, a ricin attack. The dead—as many as 15,000 in France alone, 30,000 in Europe at large—succumbed to

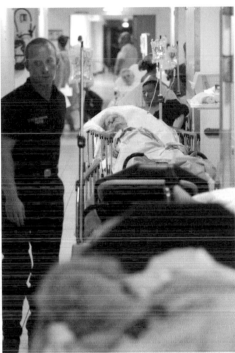

As unusually high temperatures hit Paris, France, in August 2003, children cooled off in fountains, while many elderly people, sickened by the heat, were hospitalized.

something far more primordial. They died of heat. For ten freakish days [in] August [2003] Paris became Death Valley, with temperatures surpassing 104 degrees. Nights offered no relief: On the murderous eve of August 11th, even the low temperature hovered near 80. And so they cooked. Hyperthermia. Elevated body temperature. Dehydration. Nausea, cramping, exhaustion. The elderly were the the most vulnerable. Some literally keeled over while walking up stairwells. Others—so weakened by a week and a half of extreme heat—died quietly in their apartments, announcing their passing only by the stench of their decay.

In another moment in the world's history, the massacre might have been chalked up to an "act of God." But these deaths had man's fingerprints all over them. And not simply in the stifling medieval architecture of Paris, the dearth of air conditioners, the inadequate emergency response. Man may well have been responsible for the heat itself.

Global warming. It doesn't just make the world hotter—it makes the weather more extreme. Droughts are longer, torrents heavier, flooding more severe. Heat waves are turned up to eleven. "Because of our fossil-fuel burning, we are changing the climate," says Sir John Houghton, former co-chairman of the Intergovernmental Panel on Climate Change [IPCC], the United Nations scientific organization that is literally the world authority on global warming. In 2001, the IPCC forecast that Earth would soon see "higher maximum temperatures, more hot days and heat waves"—causing increased mortality in "older age groups and the urban poor." Two years later, Europe was hit by Extreme Summer 2003. . . .

Not Just a Theory

Global warming is no longer a theory, some distant doomsday. It's all too real—and it's here now. Indeed, the only serious debate in the scientific community is not *whether* we are changing the climate, but *how much* and *how bad will it get*. "Climate-change scientists are of one mind on this," says Sir David King, chief science adviser to the British government. "We're no longer discussing whether the global warming we're observing is related to human effects. Fossil-fuel burning is leading to significant climate change. The predictions made back in the 1890s are believed to be coming true."

And so it begins. Our world is measurably warmer—by a full degree in the last century, more than twice that near the poles—and getting hotter. The twentieth century was the hottest of the last millennium. Nineteen of the twenty hottest years on record have occurred since 1980, with 2003 the third-hottest year ever. The warming projected by the IPCC for this century—between 2.5 and 10.4 degrees—is unprecedented in the last 10,000 years. As we drive our cars and burn coal to light our homes, we force more carbon dioxide, the primary greenhouse gas, into the atmosphere. CO_2 concentrations are higher than they've been at any time since giant carnivorous kangaroos roamed the earth 50,000 years

A Disturbing Future

A future of more severe storms and floods along the world's increasingly crowded coastlines is likely.

United Nations Framework Convention on Climate Change, "Feeling the Heat," http://unfccc.int/2860.php, September 24, 2005.

ago. The IPCC concluded in 2001 that "most of the observed warming in the last fifty years" could be blamed on human activity.

A Disturbing Trend

Some would write off the French heat wave as a tragic blip. Ditto that 2003 was the hottest European summer in 500 years. Ditto that it came so quickly after extreme floods soaked the continent in 2002, forcing the evacuation of 50,000 in Prague. But these are hardly the only blips. In March [2003] Brazil was hit by its first-ever hurricane. [In] June [2003] a heat wave scorched India with twenty-seven consecutive days of 120-degree temperatures, killing nearly 2,000. Flooding in China that used to hit once every twenty years now recurs almost annually; a deluge [in] August [2003] left 4 million homeless. The American West is suffering years of record drought, and [in] May [2003] 502 tornadoes struck the Midwest—103 more than the previous monthly record. A retractable barrier built to protect London from floods was expected to be used once every three years. In 2000, it was used twenty-four times.

"One event is not evidence," says Houghton. "But if you get these happening rather often, then you begin to see a trend."

Take the world's glaciers. Kilimanjaro's permanent ice cap in Kenya—Hemingway's "Snows of Kilimanjaro"—is melting at an astonishing rate. In fifteen years it will completely disappear. Four glaciers in Venezuela already have. "These glaciers are very much like the canaries once used in coal mines," says Lonnie Thompson, a glacier scientist at Ohio State University. "They're an indicator of massive changes taking place in the climate in the tropics."

But it's not just the tropics. Ice is in retreat worldwide. Glacier National Park in Montana will be namesake-free by 2030. In Alaska, where temperatures have soared four degrees in the last fifty years, the state's permafrost—*perma* frost—is thawing. . . .

An Indian woman searches for water near a dried-up lake in the drought-stricken state of Gujarat. Drought is a continuing challenge for millions of people across India.

Preventing Catastrophe

The world's leading scientists agree that it's already too late to halt global warming entirely. "We can't prevent some damage," says Stephen Schneider, co-director of the Center for Environmental Science and Policy at Stanford University. Even if we were to magically end CO_2 emissions tomorrow, the gases that we've already unleashed will continue to raise temperatures for another 150 years. "That's unpreventable," Schneider says.

By starting now, however, we can still prevent many of the more catastrophic effects of global warming. If we're ambitious, we may be able to keep the concentration of carbon in the atmosphere below 450 parts per million—only 70 ppm higher than today. That should be enough, scientists say, to prevent the Greenland and West Antarctic ice sheets from melting and eventually submerging the world's coastal areas. . . .

"Slowing it down matters," Schneider says. "The faster and harder you push on the ecological system, the more harm to nature—and the more the likelihood of surprise."

What kind of surprises? . . .

"I'm talking about *nasty* surprises," he adds. "Are there more of those lurking? Undoubtedly."

Analyze the essay:

1. Take note of the descriptive anecdote that Dickinson uses to open his essay. What details of sight, sound, touch, taste, and smell do you find to be most compelling? What does the use of such details lend to his essay?

2. Dickinson argues that fossil fuel emissions from car engines, coal burning, and other kinds of energy consumption by humans has increased the rate of global warming over the past century. What evidence does Dickinson provide to support his viewpoint? In your opinion, how effective is his use of evidence?

Global Warming May Not Be the Cause of Extreme Weather

Christopher Lingle

Christopher Lingle is a professor of economics at Francisco Marroquin University in Guatemala. In the following viewpoint Lingle questions the idea that global temperatures are rising and causing an increase in severe weather. For example, he explains that extreme weather conditions could simply be more widely reported than they were in the past. In addition, improved technology allows more people to live in areas that are naturally prone to extreme weather, increasing human vulnerability to disasters, notes Lingle. Most significantly, he points out, no solid proof exists that the use of fossil fuels causes climate change, or even that global warming is necessarily a bad thing.

Consider the following questions:

1. According to Lingle, why are land temperatures rising?
2. How might greenhouse gases actually induce cooling, according to the author?
3. In Lingle's opinion, why do environmental activists and politicians prefer to have people believe in catastrophic scenarios?

Extreme weather is making headlines. Record summer temperatures in Europe and a large number of heat-related deaths in India joined news about severe flooding

In 2003 a family of villagers walks with their belongings through floodwaters in Matara, Sri Lanka.

in Bangladesh, China, and Sri Lanka. And an unusual number of tornados in the United States have been reported.

For its part the UN World Meteorological Organization (WMO) suggests that global warming is linked to these events. It also declared that extremes in weather and climate are setting new records and the number of such extreme events has been rising. (The [George W.] Bush administration plans to spend $103 million to study global climate change.)

Raising Questions

But these reports raise many questions. As the director of the WMO admitted, the results reflect the fact that monitoring and communication of weather conditions are better than ever before. It turns out that the only certainty is that reporting of extremes is more common, even if the extremes are not.

As it is, little attention is paid to the fact that some of the vulnerability to extreme weather arises from changing human population patterns. Over the years, foreign aid and emergency disaster relief encouraged the building of slums or suburban housing in flood plains. Similarly, air conditioning allows more people to live comfortably in areas subject to hurricanes and cyclones.

In its report, the WMO notes that global averages for land and sea surface temperatures in May [2003] are the second highest since records began in 1880. However, temperatures in the upper atmosphere were not reported. This is no slight oversight. For global warming to be truly global, atmospheric temperatures would also have to be rising. But there is no evidence that air temperatures have risen to match the reports of rising ground temperatures.

Consider the fact that surface temperatures have been increasingly recorded in urban areas or airports that have much more concrete and asphalt than they had even a few decades back. All other things constant, it would be surprising if temperatures taken in such "hot spots" did not increase.

Such alternative explanations tend to be ignored. And so it has become an article of faith that burning fossil fuels increases greenhouse gases (GHG) that lock in heat and cause global warming.

An Uncertain Science

Contrary to conventional wisdom, scientific understanding of climate change remains quite unsettled. In particular, it is not clear that observed global warming trends are significant or relevant to the long-term survival of life on earth. Nor is it clear that attempts to reduce greenhouse gases will offset other factors that influence climate. Indeed, there is a strong correlation between sunspot activity and temperature variations.

In all events, GHGs are not the only possible source of warming trends and not necessarily the most important. Weather and climate patterns depend on influences from oceans and other water systems, the variability of solar radiation, volcanic aerosols, and greenhouse gas emissions, as well as clouds and water vapor, just to name a few.

The UN Intergovernmental Panel on Climate Change (IPCC) considers at least 12 conditions that could change climate. Of these, only greenhouse gases have come under the close scrutiny of the scientific community. Uncertainty over the influence of the other conditions means that they could worsen the warming trend or reduce it or cancel it out completely.

A Cooling Haze?

A report released by the United Nations identified a two-mile-thick "Asian Brown Cloud" that is blamed partly on greenhouse gases. However, an examination of the effects of this enormous blanket of haze found that it counteracts global warming by shading land areas that it covers. So, it turns out that sometimes GHGs can induce cooling.

Stayskal. © 2002 by Knight Ridder/Tribune Information Services. Reproduced by permission.

This satellite image of central China clearly shows the "Asian Brown Cloud," a vast blanket of pollution caused by greenhouse gas emissions from cars and other sources.

This is not the only beneficial property of GHGs. It is also overlooked that CO_2, one of the most infamous carbon-based GHGs, is actually plant food that is converted into oxygen.

Greenhouse Politics

Meanwhile, most economic analyses indicate that mandating reductions in greenhouse gases will cause significant harm of which we can be certain, in exchange for uncertain benefits. Our incomplete understanding of the climate system raises questions over the effectiveness of local or regional responses to perceptions about global climate change.

Since global climate history reveals wide fluctuations over the earth's life, it is important to choose an appropriate time frame for reference to allow for reasonable comparisons. Most climate models used by the IPCC cover the last 1,000 years of climate variation. However, most of the data are estimates because surface temperature data have been recorded for only about 150 years. And weather balloon readings have been collected for 30 years, while satellite readings span less than 20 years.

It turns out that greenhouse politics suffers from a tendency to exaggerate. Environmental activists use worst-case scenarios that reflect their own biases to raise funds to support their causes. Politicians have a vested interest in citizens' believing in catastrophic scenarios that make it easier to levy new taxes, since guilt or uncertain risks make them more willing to surrender more of their income.

While the perceptions of the general public are influenced by these biases, rising incomes also lead to increased demand for higher environmental quality. Politicians and bureaucrats have tended to respond by imposing stricter environmental regulations, with violations receiving ever wider media coverage. In turn, there has been a misperception that environmental quality is worsening when it may actually be improving or perhaps remaining unchanged.

Even if global temperatures are rising, we do not really understand why. Neither do we know if nor how soon the worst-case scenarios might occur. Even their ultimate consequences remain uncertain.

Analyze the essay:

1. In this viewpoint, the author argues that no proof exists that severe weather is caused by global warming. He counters the opinion of the previous author, who believes that global warming is responsible for an increase in extreme weather. After reading both viewpoints, which do you find more persuasive? Identify a particular technique or argument that helped sway you.

2. Lingle presents several explanations for recent weather extremes. What are these "causes"? Does Lingle persuade you that these causes may explain weather extremes? Explain.

Global Warming Threatens Polar Life

Current Events

Global warming is having a drastic effect on the climate of the Arctic, reports *Current Events* in the following essay. Rising temperatures endanger polar bears, seals, and other animals that live in icy environments. The native peoples of the Arctic are also threatened by melting permafrost. It destroys their homes and creates economic strife as hunting and foraging become more difficult. Furthermore, the authors point out, melting ice could cause sea levels to rise, resulting in a flooding of coastal areas around the world. *Current Events* is a weekly news journal.

Consider the following questions:

1. How much of the Arctic summer sea ice could melt by the end of this century, according to *Current Events?*
2. What creates the greenhouse effect, according to the authors?
3. According to this viewpoint, what opportunities might arise as an effect of global warming?

Roaming the ice with their snow-colored fur, polar bears are the kings of cool. They like to chill out on giant ice floes, take icy dips in the frigid seas, and snack on seals and any other creature that fits their fancy. At the top of the Arctic food chain, polar bears are 1,000-pound beasts nobody messes with. But there's danger underfoot for the white wonders. A new report by an international team of

Current Events, "On Thin Ice: Global Warming Spells Big Trouble at the Top of the World," vol. 104, December 17, 2004, p. 1. Copyright © 2004 by the Weekly Reader Corp. Reproduced by permission.

Shrinking Western Ice Sheets

Recent satellite data suggest that the Pine Island glacier in West Antarctica has retreated up to three miles from 1992 to 2000.

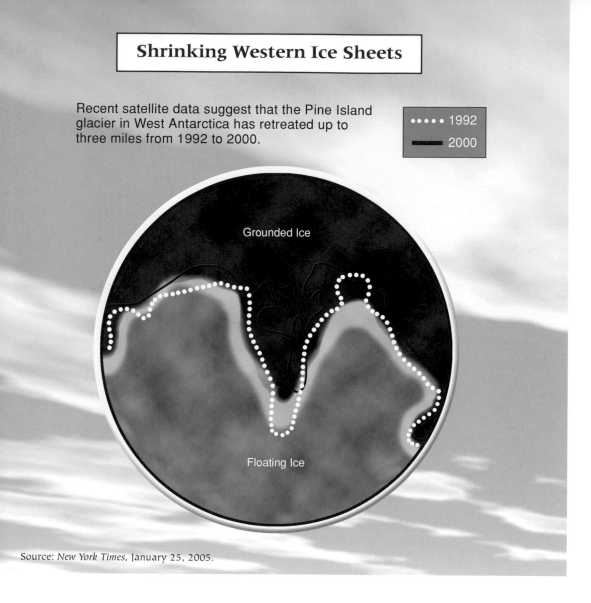

····· 1992
▬▬ 2000

Grounded Ice

Floating Ice

Source: *New York Times*, January 25, 2005.

300 scientists warns that the polar bear's icy habitat is melting away—fast.

Presented recently in Iceland's capital, the Arctic Climate Impact Assessment (ACIA) report states that rising temperatures are melting the polar ice cap at an alarming rate. At least half the summer sea ice in the Arctic is projected to have melted by the end of this century, along with a large portion of the Greenland ice sheet. The region is expected to warm an additional 7 to 13 degrees by 2100.

The result of the meltdown could be an ecological disaster that spells the end of polar bears and many other Arctic animals. The changing climate also could have a profound effect on the world. "The Arctic is experiencing some of the most rapid and severe climate change on Earth," said Robert Corell, chair of the ACIA. "The impacts of climate change on the region and globe are projected to increase substantially in the years to come. The Arctic is really warming now. These areas provide a bellwether of what's coming to planet Earth," he said.

The report was funded by the United States and the seven other nations that border the Arctic region: Russia, Canada, Iceland, Sweden, Norway, Denmark, and Finland. It took scientists four years to compile the report, which included results from five different computer models to project the effects of Arctic warming.

It's Getting Hot in Here

Scientists blame the Arctic meltdown on global warming, or the gradual increase of Earth's average temperature. Climate change is nothing new. But many scientists are concerned that natural temperature fluctuations are being aggravated by human activity. Many vehicles, power plants, and factories emit greenhouse gases. Those gases, such as carbon dioxide, trap heat from the sun close to Earth, creating the greenhouse effect.

> ## Endangered Animals
>
> The Arctic Ocean [may] become ice-free much of the year, imperiling populations of walrus and seal that feed on creatures living on the ice.
>
> Bruce E. Johansen, "Arctic Heat Wave," *Progressive*, October 2001.

Many scientists believe that the biggest danger of accelerated global warming in the Arctic is the resulting rise in sea levels. The ACIA report states that the annual average amount of sea ice has decreased about 8 percent in the past 30 years. The total loss—roughly 386,100 square miles—represents an area bigger than Arizona and Texas combined.

If Greenland's ice sheet continues to melt at its current rate, "the consequences would be catastrophic,"

The Arctic animals this Inuit hunts for food face extinction because of global warming.

Jonathan Overpeck, director of the Institute for the Study of Planet Earth at the University of Arizona, told *National Geographic*. The ACIA report warns that a complete melting of the Greenland ice sheet could cause sea levels to rise by 23 feet. Even a partial melting would cause a 3-foot rise in global sea levels. Computer models show that low-lying coastal areas in Florida and Louisiana would be flooded. A 1.5-foot rise could cause the coastline to move 150 feet inland. That means "no more Mardi Gras," said Overpeck.

Feeling the Heat

The study also warns of dire consequences for the people and animals that call the Arctic home. "This is very likely to have devastating consequences for some Arctic animal species . . . and for the local people for whom these animals are a primary food source. Should the Arctic Ocean become ice-free in summer, it is likely that polar bears and some seal species would be driven toward extinction," the ACIA report states.

Polar bears use the sea ice as platforms from which to hunt for seals, fish, and other food. Seals rest and give birth on the ice. A continued rise in temperature would affect other animals as well. Caribou, reindeer, and snowy owls, for example, would be forced to move farther north into a narrower range as their native habitat gets too warm.

Even the indigenous people of the Arctic are feeling the heat. "Our homes are threatened by storms and melting permafrost; our livelihoods are threatened by changes

Weddell seals and other Arctic species depend on an icy environment in order to thrive and propagate.

to the plants and animals we harvest," said Chief Gary Harrison of the Arctic Athabaskan Council.

Residents of Shishmaref, Alaska, are slowly losing their villages to storm-driven waves that were once restrained by the Chukchi Sea's ice cover. Many people have moved their homes to escape the advancing waters.

On the Bright Side?

The ACIA report wasn't all bad news, however. "There will be new opportunities too," Pal Prestrud, vice chair of the ACIA, told the *Philadelphia Inquirer*. The report noted that fisheries would be more productive with shorter winters. Less ice would make it easier for ships to navigate the Northwest Passage and other treacherous sea routes. And oil companies would have easier access to oil and gas deposits beneath the Arctic tundra.

Still, for many scientists, the good produced by global warming doesn't outweigh the bad. Susan Joy Hassol, the author of the ACIA report, told *National Geographic* that global warming must be slowed. "A climate system is like a supertanker, you can't turn on a dime, so you have to turn the wheel now to avoid that iceberg [far] ahead."

Analyze the essay:

1. *Current Events* discusses several catastrophes that could occur as Arctic ice melts, including a drastic rise in sea levels and the extinction of polar bears and seals. Yet the authors also point out some of the possible benefits of having less ice in the Arctic. Do you think the mention of these opportunities undermines the article's main point? Why or why not?
2. Reread the introduction and the conclusion of this viewpoint. What techniques do the authors use to spark a reader's interest?

Global Warming Is Not a Threat to Polar Life

Philip Stott

A large section of an Antarctic ice shelf collapsed into the sea in 2002. Environmentalists then issued warnings about the effects of global climate change. In the following viewpoint Philip Stott argues that shifting polar ice might not be caused by global warming. While some ice sheets have been melting, others are growing thicker, and some Antarctic regions have actually grown colder in recent years. He suggests Earth could even be entering another ice age. Such dramatic environmental changes are a normal part of life on this planet, the author explains. Stott is a former professor of biogeography at London University.

Consider the following questions:

1. What is an ice shelf, according to Stott? Why does the collapse of an ice shelf not raise sea levels?
2. Why is it difficult to interpret ecological trends in Antarctica, in the author's view?
3. How long has the planet been in its current interglacial period, according to Stott? How long do most interglacial periods last?

The dramatic demise of the Larsen B ice shelf in Antarctica in March 2002 has been embraced by environmentalists and commentators who warn of human-induced "global warming." After all, the ice shelf was 200 meters thick, with a surface area three times the size of

Hong Kong. Around 500 billion tons of ice collapsed in less than a month. How could President George W. Bush ignore such evidence of our guilt with regard to climate change?

An ice shelf is a floating extension of the continental ice that covers the landmass of Antarctica. Larsen B was one of five shelves that have been monitored by scientists. The U.S.-based National Snow and Ice Data Center described its break-up as "the largest single event in a series of retreats by ice shelves in the peninsula over the last 30 years."

A Wake-Up Call?

One worry can be dismissed immediately: Having been a shelf—a floating part of an ice sheet, rather than over land—it does not raise sea levels upon melting. Yet the collapse has proved to be a perfect natural disaster for the "Apocalypse Now" school of journalism. It is now perfect-

In January 2002 the Antarctic Larsen B Ice Shelf began breaking up. Its collapse, however, has had no measurable effect on sea levels.

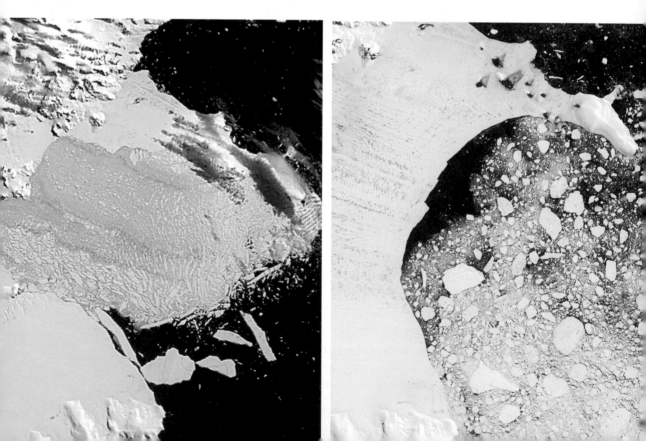

ly clear that we are all doomed and that this is the wake-up call for urgent action on greenhouse gas emissions, automobiles, industry, and virtually everything else to do with economic growth.

Unfortunately, the story isn't quite so straightforward. Antarctica illustrates the complexities behind understanding climate change, and it provides little support for a simplistic myth of human-induced "global warming." In fact this scare is reminiscent of a much-hyped *New York Times* story in 2001 that "leads" of open water in ice fields near the North Pole filled cruise passengers with a "sense of alarm" about impending climate disasters. But icebreakers are always searching for "leads" to make their way through the ice, and after a long summer of 24-hour days it is not unusual to find them all over the place, especially after strong winds break up the winter ice. Sorry, the North Pole isn't disappearing—and neither is the South Pole.

Thickening Ice

Research on the West Antarctic Ice Sheet has shown precisely the opposite trend seen at Larsen B, namely that this ice sheet may be getting thicker, not thinner. Most scientists think that the sheet has probably been retreating, spasmodically, for around the last 10,000 years, but instead of the rate accelerating in recent years, it now appears to have halted its retreat. There is evidence that the ice sheet in the Ross Sea area is growing by as much as 26.8 gigatons per year, particularly on a part of the ice sheet known as Stream C.

This demonstrates the innate complexity of Antarctica as a continent. In reality, it has many "climates," and many geomorphological and glaciological regimes. It does not respond to change, whatever the direction, in a single, unitary fashion. Geomorphological and ecological trends are thus very difficult to interpret in a linear way.

A Colder Climate

One trend has been toward a colder climate. Over the last 50 years, the temperatures in the interior appear to have been falling. University of Illinois researchers have reported, in *Nature,* on temperature records covering a broad area of Antarctica. Their measurements show "a net cooling on the Antarctic continent between 1966 and 2000." Indeed, some regions, like the McMurdo Dry Valleys, the largest ice-free area, appear to have cooled between 1986 and 1999 by as much as two degrees centigrade per decade. As the researchers wryly comment, "Continental Antarctic cooling, especially the seasonality of cooling, poses challenges to models of climate and ecosystem change."

At the same time that parts of the continent are cooling, it's hardly surprising to see some ice melting. We are currently emerging—granted in a somewhat jerky fashion—out of the Little Ice Age that ended around 1880. It's to be expected that some parts of Antarctica like Larsen B are retreating. Yet we seem to be shocked at this perfectly natural event. When will we recognize the basic truth that change, both evolutionary and catastrophic, is the norm on our ever-restless planet?

Extreme environmentalists and sensationalist journalists pretend that every environmental event is of our own making. If only. We don't have that much control over Mother Nature. While we've been busy gabbing about global warming, the planet may be moving in the opposite direction.

Research indicates that the Ross Ice Shelf, located at the southernmost navigable point on the planet, is becoming thicker.

Our current interglacial period is already 10,000 years old. No interglacial period during the last half-million years has persisted for more than 12,000 years. Most have had life spans of only 10,000 years or less. Statistically, therefore, we are due to slither into the next glacial period.

Despite a short-term rise in temperature of around 0.6 degrees centigrade over the last 150 years, the long-term temperature trend remains, overall, one of cooling. It may not be too long, therefore, before we see the ice spreading again. At worst, the emission of greenhouse gases is only likely to produce a super interglacial period; at worst, withdrawing gases might help to speed the descent into the next glacial period. And what would you prefer, a warmer or a colder world?

Analyze the essay:

1. How would you describe the tone of Stott's essay? Explain.
2. In his essay Stott uses several strong modifiers to describe reporters and scientists he disagrees with, referring to them as the "'Apocalypse Now' school of journalism," "extreme environmentalist," and "sensationalist journalists." In what way do these descriptions influence your opinion of those who believe that global warming is a threat? Do you think this type of writing has a positive or a negative effect on the author's argument?

Fixing Global Warming Will Require Global Sacrifice

Richard D. Lamm and Buie Seawell

In the following viewpoint Richard D. Lamm and Buie Seawell argue that global warming threatens all of humanity and demands immediate action. Societies have failed to take such action, however, because difficult lifestyle changes are required to confront global warming. The authors conclude that preventing a future global warming catastrophe must become a unifying cause for humanity. Lamm is a public policy professor at the University of Denver; Seawell is a business professor at the same university.

Consider the following questions:

1. What environmental evidence reveals the current effects of global warming, in the authors' opinion?
2. According to historian Barbara Tuchman, quoted by the authors, why is it hard for leaders to respond to new realities?
3. How many years will it take today's pollution to impact the environment as greenhouse gases, according to Lamm and Seawell?

Global warming is not just another issue in a long line of environmental problems that have received attention starting with Earth Day, 1970. With honor and respect to all the great environmental victories and to the people who fought for them, we feel that global warming will take a revolution in the way we see ourselves.

Adequately confronting global warming will require as much change from us as was required during the transition to the industrial revolution. We must, in effect, learn to live in a whole new world.

Evidence of Global Warming

While there is still much uncertainty about what impact global warming will have upon the earth, we know enough now to start the journey to sustainability. Evidence of global warming is sufficient to hold policymakers guilty

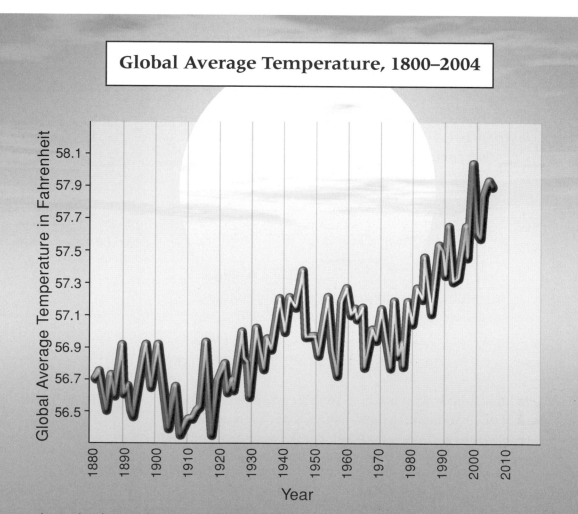

Global Average Temperature, 1800–2004

Source: The Woods Hole Research Center, www.whrc.org.

of public-policy malpractice if they fail to act immediately and vigorously. History's judgment will be harsh on those who ignore such clear warning signs.

Our oceans are warming, our ice caps and glaciers are melting, our soils are eroding, our rainforests are shrinking, our ocean coral is dying, our fisheries are being depleted and more and more species are disappearing. We are told by the National Academy of Sciences, the Royal Society and most of the living Nobel Prize winners that global warming is a reality that we must take seriously. Even the Pentagon, hardly a historic voice for the environment, has issued a report, "An Abrupt Climate Change Scenario and Its Implications for US National Security," laying out a series of possible nation-threatening scenarios for global warming.

Thought to be caused by global warming, coral bleaching could lead to the extinction of many coral species.

Beyond Imagination

How can anyone read these reports and return to business as usual?

Perhaps because the implications to our everyday lives are so immense that we'd rather not comprehend them. One reason the attack on 9/11 succeeded was that the possibility of crashing planes into skyscrapers was almost beyond imagination.

Likewise with global warming: Trying to imagine a world without growing petroleum use or traditional ways of growing the economy, or where human population must shrink rather than grow, comes close to the unimaginable. Historian Barbara Tuchman observed how hard it is for those in charge to react to new realities: "When information is relayed to policymakers, they respond in terms of what is already inside their heads and consequently make policy less to fit the facts than to fit the baggage that has accumulated since childhood."

The Need to Act

We are making a mess of the earth; we are fouling our nest and we have to act decisively and against our immediate inclinations.

Ian McEwan, "Let's Talk About Climate Change," www.opendemocracy.net, April 21, 2005.

The Tragedy in the Commons

It is also immensely difficult to see our individual place within the ecological whole. The most cited article in the history of *Science* magazine helps us understand why. Garrett Hardin's "The Tragedy in the Commons" concluded that when natural resources are held in common, free and available to all for the taking, people steadily increase their exploitation of the common resources until they are exhausted. Every participant in the tragedy pleads "not guilty." But the entire system moves toward disaster.

The poet W.H. Auden wrote, "All life is the question of whether or not to have children, after you've already had them." It is hard for us to see how our automobiles, our airplane travel or our third or fourth child will affect the environment when they bring us so much pleasure, but the impact is shared worldwide.

We do not recognize the lifetimes it takes to correct environmental damage or to reverse the damage already done. So it is a surprise to realize that the exhaust from President Kennedy's automobile on the day he was assassinated still hasn't fully played out its environmental impact. It takes

Environmentalists in Germany rally to demand that the industrialized nations of the world adopt policies to help reduce greenhouse gas emissions.

perhaps 60 or 70 years for today's pollution to reach full impact as greenhouse gases. Like a car breaking down, it will take us a significant and perhaps fatal amount of time to break down our industrial society. It will require foresight not historically present in humankind.

A Clash of Civilizations

What we treat as just another environmental issue is more accurately a clash of civilizations. It is the shift from identifying individual polluters to be stopped to the issue of all of our lifestyles. We can only observe how nearsighted it is that so many people today focus on cultural and religious differences between the West and Islam, when human civilization itself stands on the brink of collapse.

Is it naive to hope that—like the appearance of an Earthbound asteroid or the invasion of extraterrestrial aliens in all those countless, trite science fiction films—global warming may be the common cause that finally unites the human enterprise? Whatever it takes, we must begin to focus on the one environmental issue that threatens us all.

Analyze the essay:

1. The authors speculate on reasons why the threat of global warming is not being seriously confronted. What are these reasons or causes? Do you agree that humans "lack the foresight" to reverse global warming? Explain.
2. Lamm and Seawell describe the global warming issues as a "clash of civilizations." What do you think they mean by this?

Global Warming Will Be Beneficial

Dennis Avery

A warmer planet provides many benefits, contends Dennis Avery in the following selection. In the past, he notes, periods of cooler weather have led to droughts, poor harvests, and famine. But warmer temperatures bring more sunshine and rainfall, boosting crop production and reducing hunger, he points out. In addition, a warmer climate tends to stabilize weather patterns, resulting in fewer weather-related deaths, he concludes. Avery is the director for the Center for Global Food Issues at the Hudson Institute, a public policy think tank.

Consider the following questions:
1. How many years does it take the earth to go through a climate cycle, according to Avery?
2. What happened during the coldest part of the Little Ice Age, according to the author?
3. According to Avery, how does warmer weather help the growth of food crops?

Only in the past 20 years have scientists begun to understand that the Earth has a moderate, persistent 1,500-year climate cycle that creates warmings and coolings. Sunspot records and the isotopes of carbon, oxygen and beryllium trapped in ice cores and cave stalagmites indicate that this process is driven by a small cycle in the sun's radiance.

Dennis Avery, "Climate Forecast: Warm and Sunny," www.cgfi.org, May 19, 2005. Reproduced by permission.

The Earth's climate is more stable during warming periods. The warming heats the polar regions more than the equatorial regions, reducing temperature differences and thus reducing the power of storms. For instance, Chinese court records indicate far fewer floods and droughts during the Roman Warming of the first century and the Medieval Warming of the 12th century than during the intervening cold Dark Ages and the recent Little Ice Age.

At the latitudes of New York and Paris, temperatures during the warm periods rise about 2° C above the mean for 500 to 750 years. Then they fall abruptly about 2 degrees below the mean for a similar period. Thus, the Earth's climate is always warming or cooling.

Hot and Cold Cycles

Scientists first noted that the Roman and Medieval warmings were part of a much longer pattern when Greenland ice cores, first brought up in 1984, provided 250,000 years of climate history. Evidence of the 1,500-year climate cycles has since been found in Antarctic glaciers, in the seabed sediments of four oceans, in ancient tree rings, and in cave stalagmites on all the continents and New Zealand. But the 1,500-year cycles were too long and too moderate for ancient peoples without thermometers and written records to discern.

In Europe, the Roman Warming of the First Century lasted from 200 B.C. to 600 A.D. It allowed grapes and olives to be grown farther north, and good rains allowed the Romans to buy abundant grain from across the Mediterranean in North Africa. The Roman Warming was followed by the cold Dark Ages (600 to 950 A.D.). Weather is far less stable during the cold phases of the climate cycle. Widespread droughts and storms drove hordes of hungry barbarians to assault the granaries of the collapsing Roman Empire.

The Medieval Warming prevailed from about A.D. 950 to 1300, bringing ample sunshine, milder storms and longer growing seasons. Food harvests were so good that

A scientist examines a core sample taken from the Greenland Ice Sheet containing sediments (right) that provide invaluable information about climate cycles.

Britain's population rose from an estimated 1.4 million people in the late 11th century to 5 million in 1300. Europe's total population increased from 40 million to 60 million—during a period when temperatures rose higher than today's.

The Little Ice Age

From 1300 to 1850, the planet shifted into the Little Ice Age. The good weather ended abruptly. During the summer of 1315, incessant sheets of rain fell from May to August throughout Europe, washing away much of the topsoil and beating crops to the ground. In late summer, the weather turned unseasonably cold, and the soft kernels of the few surviving grain plants were attacked by

Despite the lack of rain in this North Dakota cornfield, farmers can still grow crops using special methods that preserve soil moisture and boost crop harvests.

fungus. Across northern Europe, harvests were disastrous, and famine set in. . . .

In the coldest part of the Little Ice Age, during the 16th and 17th centuries, famine struck repeatedly. The combination of famine and bubonic plague reduced Britain's population from 5 million to 4 million, and life expectancy dropped from 48 years to 38. The population of the Indian subcontinent dropped from 200 million in A.D. 1200 to 140 million in 1600. . . .

The Healthy Effects of Warming

History and science both tell us that a warmer planet has beneficial effects on food production. It results in longer growing seasons, more sunshine, and more rainfall, while summertime high temperatures change very little. In addition, a warmer planet means milder winters and fewer crop-killing frosts in the late spring and early fall.

The present warming trend has not resulted in agricultural water shortages. Rather, rainfall is currently increasing moderately over most of the world. This is not surprising. Global warming evaporates more water from the oceans, and it falls back down to earth in a reinvigorated hydrological cycle. . . . Continued warming should enhance rainfall, rather than suppress it. And even if some areas do experience greater aridity under warmer conditions, both nature and humans have been through it many times before, and adapted.

Some scientists argue that global warming may actually benefit farmers, such as this Tibetan grain farmer, by increasing crop yields.

Global warming also brings additional CO_2, which acts like fertilizer for plants. As the planet warms, oceans naturally release huge tonnages of additional CO_2 that dwarf the output from our cars and factories. (Cold water can hold much more of a gas than warmer water.) For plants, it's like letting Lance Armstrong carry an oxygen tank on his racing bike.

Since 1950, during a period of global warming, these factors have helped the world's grain production soar from 700 million tons to more than 2 billion tons last year [2004].

Do Not Fear Global Warming

History shows that a warmer world is better for human health on average. It tends to boost agricultural productivity, which reduces hunger and the illnesses that inadequate nutrition help produce. In addition, weather patterns are generally more stable with fewer catastrophic weather events, and warm weather produces far fewer deaths than cold weather. These factors contribute to longer average life spans and increased human populations during climatic warm periods compared to cooler times.

From the perspective of human health, people have far more to fear from the next full Ice Age than the modest warming that most experts believe the planet will experience in the coming century.

Analyze the essay:

1. Avery provides some background about climate cycles of the past. How does this history provide support for his argument? Does his discussion of climate history engage you as a reader? Why or why not?
2. Do you find Avery's argument about the benefits of global warming to be convincing? Why or why not? Cite passages from his essay as you explain your answer.

Section Two: Model Essays and Writing Exercises

The Five-Paragraph Essay

An essay is a short piece of writing that discusses or analyzes one topic. Five-paragraph essays are a form commonly used in school assignments and tests. Every five-paragraph essay begins with an introduction, ends with a conclusion, and features three supporting paragraphs in the middle.

The Thesis Statement. The introduction includes the essay's thesis statement. The thesis statement presents the argument or point the author is trying to make about the topic. The essays in this book all have different thesis statements because they are making different arguments about global warming.

The thesis statement should be a clear statement that tells the reader what the essay will be about. A focused thesis statement helps determine what will be in the essay; the subsequent paragraphs are spent developing and supporting its argument.

The Introduction. In addition to presenting the thesis statement, a well-written introductory paragraph captures the attention of the reader and explains why the topic being explored is important. It may provide the reader with background information on the subject matter or feature an anecdote that illustrates a point relevant to the topic. It could also present startling information that clarifies the point of the essay or present a contradictory position that the essay will refute. Further techniques for writing an introduction are found later in this section.

The Supporting Paragraphs. The introduction is followed by three (or more) supporting paragraphs. These are the main body of the essay. Each paragraph presents and develops a subtopic that supports the essay's thesis statement. Each subtopic is then supported with its own facts, details, and examples. The writer can use various kinds of supporting material and details to back up the topic of each supporting paragraph. These may include statistics, quotations from people with special knowledge or expertise, historic facts, and anecdotes. A rule of writing is that specific and concrete examples are more convincing than vague, general, or unsupported assertions.

The Conclusion. The conclusion is the paragraph that closes the essay. Its function is to summarize or reiterate the main idea of the essay. It may recall an idea from the introduction or briefly examine the larger implications of the thesis. Because the conclusion is also the last chance a writer has to make an impression on the reader, it is important that it not simply repeat what has been presented elsewhere in the essay but close it in a clear, final, and memorable way.

Although the order of the essay's component paragraphs is important, they do not have to be written in that order. Some writers like to decide on a thesis and write the introductory paragraph first. Other writers like to focus first on the body of the essay and write the introduction and conclusion later.

Pitfalls to Avoid

When writing essays about controversial issues such as global warming, it is important to remember that disputes over the material are common precisely because there are many different perspectives. Remember to state your arguments in careful and measured terms. Evaluate your topic fairly—avoid overstating negative qualities of one perspective or understating positive qualities of another. Use examples, facts, and details to support any assertions you make.

The Cause-and-Effect Essay

T he previous section of this book provides samples of published persuasive writing on global warming. All are persuasive, or opinion, essays that put forth arguments about global warming. They are also either cause-and-effect essays or use cause-and-effect reasoning. This section will focus on writing your own cause-and-effect essays.

Cause and effect is a common method of organizing and explaining ideas and events. Simply put, cause and effect describes a relationship between two things in which one thing makes something else happen. The cause is the reason why something happens. The effect is what happens as a result.

A simple example would be a car not starting because it is out of gas. The lack of gas is the cause; the failure to start is the effect. Another example of cause-and-effect reasoning is found in Viewpoint One. Tim Dickinson argues that global warming has led to dramatic changes in climate. Global warming is the cause; heat waves, severe storms, and flooding are the effects.

Not all cause-and-effect relationships are as clear-cut as these two examples. It can be difficult to determine the cause of an effect, especially when talking about societywide causes and effects. For example, smoking and cancer have been long associated with each other, but not all cancer patients smoked, and not all smokers got cancer. It took decades of debate and research before the U.S. surgeon general concluded in 1964 that smoking cigarettes causes cancer (and even then, that conclusion was disputed by tobacco companies for many years thereafter). The authors of Viewpoint Three note that an increase in the average global temperature has coincided with a rapid melting of the polar ice cap. They argue that global warming is the cause and that melting Arctic ice and rising sea levels are the effects. Whether the melting of ice sheets is directly attributable to human-induced global warming, however, is a matter of ongoing debate. Creating and evaluating cause-and-effect arguments involve both collecting evidence and exercising critical thinking.

Types of Cause-and-Effect Essays

In general, there are three types of cause-and-effect essays. In one type, many causes can contribute to a single effect. Supporting paragraphs examine one specific cause. For example, Christopher Lingle in Viewpoint Two argues that there are several different reasons why the planet appears to be experiencing more extreme weather recently. The causes he describes include improved monitoring of weather conditions, increased housing in areas subject to floods and hurricanes, variations in solar radiation, and exaggeration on the part of environmental activists. The ultimate effect of these multiple factors is, in Lingle's opinion, a mistaken conclusion on the part of the public that global warming is creating severe weather.

Another type of cause-and-effect essay examines multiple effects from a single cause. The thesis posits that one event or circumstance has multiple results. An example from this volume is found in Viewpoint Five by Richard D. Lamm and Buie Seawell. Part of their argument is that humankind's inability to see itself as connected to its environment has led to several negative effects, including the misuse of resources, global warming, and ecological damage.

A final type of cause-and-effect essay is one that examines a series of causes and effects—a "chain of events" in which each link is both the effect of what happened before and the cause of what happens next. The writer of Essay One provides one example. Global warming (initial cause) causes an increase in severe weather (an effect). The destruction wrought by violent weather (another cause) leads to massive evacuations (an effect). Storm evacuees (another cause) can, in turn, spread infectious diseases to populations far from the initial weather disaster (another effect). The writer concludes that the health risks associated with global warming require nations to improve their disaster-relief capabilities.

Tips to Remember

In writing argumentative essays about controversial issues such as global warming, it is important to remember that disputes over cause-and-effect relationships are part of the controversy. Global warming is a complex phenomenon that has multiple effects and causes, and people disagree over what causes what. One needs to be careful and measured when expressing arguments. Avoid overstating cause-and-effect relationships unless warranted. Words and phrases such as "it is obvious" and "always" or "never" posit an absolute causal relationship without exception. Use words that qualify the argument, such as "most likely" and "it is possible."

Another pitfall to avoid in writing cause-and-effect essays is to mistake chronology for causation. Just because event X followed event Y does not necessarily mean that X caused Y. Additional evidence may be needed, such as documented studies or similar testimony from many people. Likewise, correlation does not necessarily imply causation. Just because two events happened at the same time does not necessarily mean they are causally related. Again, additional evidence is needed to verify the cause/effect argument.

In this section, you will read some model essays on global warming that use cause-and-effect arguments and do exercises that will help you write your own.

Signal or Transition Words Found in Cause-and-Effect Essays

Writers use these words to show the relationship between cause and effect, to provide transitions between paragraphs, and to summarize key ideas in an essay's concluding paragraph.

accordingly	it then follows that
as a result of	so
because	so that
consequently	since
due to	subsequently
for	therefore
for this reason	this is how
if . . . then	thus

Global Warming Threatens Human Health

Editor's Notes This first model essay is structured as a five-paragraph "chain-of-events" cause-and-effect essay. It presents global warming as the first cause in a series of events that will have negative effects on human health. Each of the three supporting paragraphs discusses an effect of global warming, and each of these effects cause yet another effect. In the first supporting paragraph, for example, the writer argues that violent weather is one effect of global warming. Then in the second supporting paragraph, violent weather is the cause that brings about the effect of local evacuations and social disorder. Finally, in the third supporting paragraph, population displacement is seen as a potential cause of disease outbreaks. The author then concludes with a paragraph that examines the implications of the essay's thesis.

As you read this essay, pay attention to its components and how they are organized. Also note that all sources are cited using Modern Language Association (MLA) style. For more information on how to cite your sources, see Appendixes B and C.

Refers to thesis and topic sentences

Refers to supporting details

The first sentence establishes the topic of the essay—global warming.

The writer asserts an opinion about global warming in the second and third sentences.

This is the thesis statement for the essay.

Paragraph 1

Many climatologists argue that the burning of fossil fuels, such as coal and natural gas, produces greenhouse gases that will raise average global temperatures by 3° to 10°F (1.7° to 5.56°C) over the next century. While this may seem like a small amount, such a planetwide temperature increase will likely have a dramatic effect on Earth's climate. Shifts in temperature zones, rising sea levels, and changing storm patterns will present serious challenges unless humankind cuts back on activities that produce planet-warming greenhouse gases. In fact, many concerned scientists speculate that these climate changes could set off a life-threatening chain of events.

Paragraph 2

Bouts of extreme weather would be the first "link" in this chain of events. A warmer atmosphere coupled with rising ocean temperatures could bring an increase in floods, tornadoes, and hurricanes, as well as heat waves, droughts, and wildfires. The climate of the 1990s—the hottest decade on record thus far—seems to bear out the warnings that weather becomes more severe as Earth's temperature rises. The year 1998 began with an ice storm that left 4 million people without power in Quebec and in the northeastern United States. For the first time, rain forests in Brazil and Mexico caught fire as droughts encroached into inland regions of Latin America. In 1999 a super-cyclone in eastern India claimed ten thousand lives, and winter mudslides and rains in Venezuela killed fifteen thousand people.

The second sentence is the topic sentence for the first supporting paragraph.

The writer provides details to support the topic sentence.

Paragraph 3

In addition to causing massive numbers of injuries and deaths, violent weather destroys shelter and health services, contaminates water supplies, and halts food production. A major challenge that such destruction poses is population movement, as large numbers of evacuees seek food, water, medical care, and shelter—often moving to already populated areas with limited resources. According to Jonathan Patz of the Johns Hopkins Bloomberg School of Public Health in Baltimore, Maryland, "The displaced population issue could be the toughest and largest public health issue of climate change, yet it is without doubt the most difficult to put our arms around."[1] Storm evacuees and migrants who are unable to find food, medical assistance, or adequate sanitation are a breeding ground for social conflicts and infectious illnesses, Patz and other public-health experts note.

The first sentence notes the effects of violent weather on survivors, thereby providing a transition from the previous paragraph.

This is the topic sentence of the second supporting paragraph.

An expert is quoted to provide support.

The final sentence previews the topic of the following paragraph.

Paragraph 4

Infectious diseases may be easier to contain in developed nations, where more readily available medicines and vaccines could thwart a dangerous outbreak. But in poorer nations, outbreaks of cholera, typhoid fever, influenza, infectious diarrhea—illnesses that are often spurred by extreme weather events and their aftermath—can spread from storm refugees to populations far from the initial catastrophe. One disturbing possibility is that emerging infectious diseases, such as Ebola and illnesses that have not yet been discovered, could find new niches in populations that have no immunities to them. Dangerous epidemics could ensue.

This is the paragraph's topic sentence and the final "effect" in the essay.

A major health threat is mentioned late in the essay to provide a powerful punch before the conclusion.

The author concludes by discussing the implications of the essay's thesis.

Paragraph 5

The risks of global warming demand action. While nations should work together to cut down on greenhouse gases, they must also find a way to meet the challenges posed by extreme weather events. According to environmental health specialist Carlos Corvalan, "Countries will need to take measures as early as possible to adapt to the potential changes, including changes to the health sector and delivery of health services."[2] World leaders need to enhance disaster-relief capabilities while striving to curb the pollution that contributes to global warming.

Notes

1. Quoted in Agnew, Bruce. "Planet Earth, Getting Too Hot for Health?" *Bulletin of the World Health Organization* Nov. 2001.

2. Quoted in Agnew. "Planet Earth."

Exercise A: Create an Outline from an Existing Essay

It often helps to create an outline of the five-paragraph essay before you write it. The outline can help you organize the information, arguments, quotes, and evidence you have gathered in your research.

For this exercise, create an outline that could have been used to write the first model essay. This "reverse engineering" exercise is meant to help you become familiar with using outlines to classify and arrange information.

Part of the outline has already been started to give you an idea of the assignment.

Outline

Write the essay's thesis: Climate changes caused by global warming could set off a life-threatening chain of events.

I. Supporting argument 1: Global warming could bring an increase in severe weather.

    A. The climate of the 1990s offers evidence that weather becomes more severe as world temperatures rise.

        1. specific details about the weather of 1998

        2. specific details about the weather of 1999

    B.

        1.

        2.

II. Supporting argument 2: Destructive weather leads to evacuations, which strain the resources of nearby communities.

    A. Quote from Jonathan Patz about displaced populations.

        1.

        2.

    B. Evacuees and migrants are a breeding ground for illnesses.

        1.

        2.

III. Supporting argument 3:

    A. evidence or elaboration

        1.

        2.

    B.

        1.

        2.

    C.

        1.

        2.

Global Warming Does Not Spread Infectious Diseases

Editor's Notes This second essay, also written in five paragraphs, is an example of a multiple-cause essay. It challenges the notion that global warming might spread certain infectious diseases, an idea expressed in Essay One. Its thesis—that causes other than global warming are responsible for the spread of mosquito-borne illnesses—is stated at the end of the first paragraph.

In the next three paragraphs, the writer argues that global warming does not spread disease by discussing several other factors that contribute significantly to outbreaks of mosquito-borne illnesses. As in the first model essay, the writer integrates the opinion of experts as well as information from the works included in the bibliography of this text.

The notes in the sidebars provide questions that will help you analyze how this essay is organized.

Refers to thesis and topic sentences

Refers to supporting details

Paragraph 1

Some public health officials have expressed deep concerns that global warming will hasten the spread of infectious diseases, especially mosquito-borne illnesses such as malaria, West Nile fever, dengue fever, yellow fever, and encephalitis. Scientists at the World Health Organization, for example, claim that warmer climates are enabling disease-carrying mosquitoes to live at higher altitudes—regions that were previously too cold and unwelcoming for these insects. As these pests enter new territories, scientists hypothesize, the diseases they carry will spread. Yet some data suggest that these analysts are wrong about the disease-distributing effects of rising temperatures. Factors other than global warming play a much larger role in the spread of mosquito-borne illnesses.

The first sentence tells the reader that the essay is about global warming and illness. What do the next two sentences do?

What does the writer do to make a transition from the first three sentences to the essay's thesis statement?

History reveals that outbreaks of tropical diseases are not necessarily heat-related. During the nineteenth century, for example, the average temperature in the Western Hemisphere was about 2°F (1.1°C) cooler than today's average temperature. Yet mosquito-borne diseases were relatively common in the United States in locales as far north as New York and Minnesota. In 1878 there were one hundred thousand reported cases of yellow fever, with nearly twenty thousand cases just in the city of Memphis, Tennessee. Moreover, between 1827 and 1946, the United States endured eight pandemics of dengue fever, including five hundred thousand cases in 1922 alone. Today, however, the U.S. rates of these illnesses are very low despite a higher average national temperature. Better sanitation, pesticides, and improved medicines have greatly reduced the incidence of mosquito-borne illnesses.

What is the topic sentence of this paragraph?

The writer uses historical data to support the position taken in the topic sentence.

While improved interventions may stop the spread of tropical diseases in developed nations, some analysts maintain that poorer nations face increasingly difficult challenges because higher average temperatures allow mosquitoes to spread to more regions of the world. And people in poorer nations do not have the benefits of good sanitation and access to medicine that people in the United States often take for granted. Yet cooler temperatures do not prevent the spread of mosquitoes. According to medical entomologist Paul Reiter, many species of mosquito survive during cold spells. Reiter points out that the West Nile–carrying mosquito, *Culex pipiens*, has a natural antifreeze that enables adults to survive through a winter. In fact, Reiter explains, "The 1998–1999 winter was much colder in Volgograd, [Russia,] than in New York, but the human toll from West Nile virus was much higher in Volgograd."[1] The claim that cooler temperatures coincide with a lower rate of mosquito-borne diseases, then, is unfounded.

How does this first sentence create a transition from the second to the third paragraph?

What and where is the topic sentence in this paragraph?

What authority is cited to support the paragraph's argument?

If global warming is not the root cause of new outbreaks of West Nile fever and other mosquito-borne diseases, what is? Misguided policies can be a significant source of disease epidemics. The banning of the insecticide DDT is one example of an ill-advised policy that has led to a resurgence of malaria in several countries. Between 1934 and 1955, eighty thousand people died of malaria in Ceylon (now Sri Lanka). After using DDT to eradicate mosquitoes, Ceylon had only seventeen cases of malaria in 1963, and then DDT spraying was discontinued. By 1969, six hundred thousand cases of malaria were reported. Similarly, after South Africa stopped using DDT in 1996, malaria deaths increased by 400 percent in just four years. In the late twentieth century, many Western nations banned the use of DDT for fear that it was poisonous to birds and could cause cancer in humans. Even though scientists have recently determined that DDT is not very toxic, U.S. and European aid agencies often refuse funding to countries that use DDT. Fearing a loss of aid, many poor tropical nations have stopped using DDT, and cases of malaria have skyrocketed.

What is the topic sentence of this paragraph?

Why do you think the writer arranged the subtopics in this particular order?

Paragraph 5

The prevalence of mosquito-borne illnesses, particularly in the developing world, stems from poverty, a lack of adequate medical care and sanitation, and bad policies. Economic inequality and poor planning, not global warming, are to blame for the spread of these diseases. Instead of trying to stop climate change, world leaders should concentrate on ways to provide developing nations with clean water, screened windows, effective pesticides, and affordable medicines to combat mosquito-borne diseases.

How does the writer avoid simply restating the three supporting ideas?

Notes

1. Reiter, Paul. "The Truth About Mosquitoes and Global Warming." *21st Century Science and Technology* Winter 2003–2004.

Exercise A: Create an Outline for an Opposing Cause-and-Effect Essay

As you did for the first model essay in this section, create an outline that could have been used to write "Global Warming Does Not Spread Infectious Diseases." Be sure to identify the essay's thesis statement, its supporting ideas, and key pieces of supporting evidence that are used.

Exercise B: Create an Outline for an Opposing Persuasive Essay

The first model essay presented one point of view regarding global warming. For this exercise, your assignment is to find supporting ideas, create an outline, and ultimately write a five-paragraph multiple-cause essay that argues a contrasting view.

Part I: Find supporting ideas.

Using information from some of the six viewpoints in the previous section, write down three or more arguments to support the following thesis statement: Global warming is not responsible for severe weather. Each argument should be presented in its own paragraph and make a distinct point proving that severe weather is not related to global warming.

For each of the three ideas, write down facts or information that support it, again drawing from the viewpoints in the previous section and from the appendixes in this text. These could be

- statistical information,
- direct quotations from the articles,
- anecdotes of past events, and
- elaboration of the cause-and-effect sequence.

Example: Severe weather appears to be increasing but is actually not.

- More housing is being built on floodplains (Lingle viewpoint).

- Air conditioning enables more people to live in areas affected by extreme weather (Lingle).
- Monitoring and reporting of weather conditions have improved (Lingle).
- Thus people get the impression that there are more extreme weather events, but this is not really the case (Lingle).

- Lingle quotation: "It turns out that the only certainty is that reporting of extremes is more common, even if the extremes are not."

Part II: Place the information from Part I in outline form.

Thesis statement: Global warming is not responsible for severe weather.

I. Alternative cause A
    Details and elaboration
II. Alternative cause B
    Details and elaboration
III. Alternative cause C
    Details and elaboration

Part III: Write the arguments in paragraph form.

You now have three arguments that support the paragraph's thesis statement, as well as supporting material. Use the outline to write out your three supporting arguments in paragraph form. Be sure each paragraph has a topic sentence that states the paragraph's thesis and supporting sentences that express the facts, details, and examples that support the paragraph's argument. The paragraph may also have a concluding or summary sentence.

The Long-Term Effects of Global Warming Are Difficult to Determine

Editor's Notes The following essay illustrates a third type of cause-and-effect essay. Here the writer discusses several potential effects of global warming and concludes that the overall results of rising world temperatures are hard to predict. As with the first two model essays, the writer makes an argument, then supports it with evidence.

Unlike the first two model essays, however, this essay contains more than five paragraphs. Many ideas require more paragraphs for adequate development. Moreover, the ability to write a sustained research or position paper is a valuable skill. Learning how to develop a longer piece of writing gives you the tools you will need to advance academically. In this essay the introduction takes up two paragraphs. The first paragraph is simply a brief description of scenes from the global-warming disaster movie, *The Day After Tomorrow*. In the second paragraph, the writer discusses the significance of this movie then "knocks down" its basic premise that global warming will have sudden catastrophic results. The evidence in the following paragraphs then reveals why global warming's ultimate effects are difficult to predict.

This essay also differs from the others in that the writer considers both positive and negative effects of global warming and arrives at an opinionated conclusion about how society should address this issue. Rather than viewing global warming as a clear-cut issue—as either entirely positive or entirely negative—the author suggests that people should take the possible effects of global warming seriously without resorting to exaggerated "doomsday" predictions.

As you read the essay, consider the questions placed in the margins of these pages.

Paragraph 1

Climatologist Jack Hall is very upset. The greenhouse effect and global warming have escalated so much that the polar ice caps have melted. Football-size hail pelts Japan. Tornadoes ravage Los Angeles. A massive tidal wave drowns New York. All of a sudden, a climatic trigger is flipped and the planet is thrown into a new ice age. Blizzards blanket New Delhi as Manhattan lies buried in a massive ice field. The world is forever changed, Hall muses, because world leaders, especially the leaders of the United States, had never taken scientists' warnings about global warming seriously.

How does the writer catch the reader's attention?

Paragraph 2

This scenario, from the 2004 disaster movie *The Day After Tomorrow*, expresses the frustration that many people feel about the world's seemingly slow response to the threat of global warming. Human activities, such as the burning of fossil fuels, have released extra greenhouse gases into the atmosphere, causing a rise in the world's average temperature. Some analysts predict that this temperature rise will cause climatic change. But are the catastrophic events depicted in the movie a real possibility? Many scientists are concerned about global warming but maintain that it is difficult to specify what its effects will be. As environmental analyst Jane S. Shaw notes, "No one knows how likely the most extreme possibilities are."[1] In fact, global warming could have positive as well as negative results, making its overall long-term effects unpredictable.

What is the thesis statement of this paragraph (and essay)?

Paragraph 3

On the one hand, rising temperatures have potentially damaging effects, including hotter days in the summer, more heat waves, more droughts, and flooding due to more frequent storms and heavier rainfalls. These changes in climate could harm ecosystems and human health and livelihoods. The increasing vulnerability of populated coastlines and islands is already apparent, many analysts point out. The Pacific island nation of

How does the writer make a transition into the third paragraph?

Why is a negative effect of global warming used as the first piece of supportive detail?

Tuvalu, for example, is gradually being swallowed up by rising sea levels and encountering more frequent severe storms. Starting in 2002 its citizens began evacuating to New Zealand. In addition, the Atlantic hurricane seasons in 2004 and 2005 caused unprecedented damage to Florida and U.S. coastal regions along the Gulf of Mexico, including the destruction of 80 percent of New Orleans, a major city. Not everyone agrees that these recent extreme weather events are the result of global warming, but the aftermath of these storms has focused public concerns on the possible negative effects of rising temperatures.

Paragraph 4

"On the other hand" parallels the first sentence of the previous paragraph while also signaling that a contrasting point will be made.

On the other hand, some experts maintain that higher average temperatures might have some positive benefits. Computer models predict that global warming will lead to fewer cold waves and fewer frost days. In addition, U.S. climate studies over the latter half of the twentieth century reveal that temperature increases so far have occurred at nighttime rather than daytime and in winter rather than summer. If nights and winters become less cold, global warming could actually lengthen the growing season for crops because nighttime frosts in the spring and fall determine how long plants can grow. Warmer and longer growing seasons could enable crops to grow in more regions of the world and help to combat hunger as world population increases.

Paragraph 5

What kind of transition is used at the beginning of this paragraph?

How does the writer shift into making a point that contrasts the topic of the previous paragraph?

The prospect of longer growing seasons makes some observers optimistic. But certain regions of the world may also experience more frequent and more severe droughts. This is because global warming could change world air currents, which in turn determine which land masses are dry and which are humid. Some computer models predict that the continental interiors will become much drier. Such a scenario could have a negative effect on crop production in agricultural areas. "Much of the

United States and Canada . . . would be drier than normal," notes textbook writer Daniel D. Chiras. "If this happened, many midwestern agricultural states, now barely able to support rainfed agriculture, could suffer crippling declines in productivity."[2] Irrigation would not be able to counteract this encroaching dryness because there would be less river water and less groundwater, Chiras explains.

How does this quotation support the paragraph's topic?

Paragraph 6

However, research shows that higher carbon dioxide levels in the atmosphere—a major cause of global warming—could boost plants' ability to use water efficiently. This could help offset drought conditions. Many climatologists, moreover, stress that it is difficult to predict where droughts will occur and how severe they will be. According to the Intergovernmental Panel on Climate Change, a rise in global temperatures "translates into prospects for more severe droughts and/or floods in some places and less severe droughts and/or floods in other places."[3] This means that dry or wet conditions could occur in any specific place at any time—more extreme conditions in certain areas and relatively normal conditions in other areas. Given this changeability, drought conditions could prove challenging but not necessarily disastrous for agriculture.

What is the topic sentence in paragraph 6?

Paragraph 7

Hotter days can be disastrous for humans, however. In August 2003 Europe was hit with a ten-day heat wave that killed thirty thousand people. Most of the victims were elderly people who had no access to air conditioning in places unaccustomed to temperatures of 100°F (36.6°C). Many scientists are concerned that such deadly events will become more frequent as the average world temperature rises. On the other hand, some experts believe that global warming will decrease the overall number of cold-weather deaths. According to economist Thomas Gale Moore, "More people die of the cold than of the heat. More die in the winter than in the summer. Statistical evidence

Why is the word "disastrous" used in the first sentence here?

The writer paraphrases information from Viewpoint One in this text.

How does the evidence presented in this paragraph support the essay's thesis?

suggests that the [warmer] climate predicted for the end of the twenty-first century might reduce U.S. deaths by almost forty thousand."[4] Still others point out that cold or hot weather disasters occur only when temperatures deviate sharply from the norm. In warmer areas such as the southern United States, cold snaps lead to more deaths. But in relatively cool regions like Europe, very high temperatures can cause deaths. Thus, some say, adjusting to global warming will likely require the use of technology that helps people live in a hotter climate.

Paragraph 8

What is the last paragraph's topic sentence?

How does the writer incorporate the essay's introduction into the conclusion?

The effects of global warming are, apparently, unpredictable. Many scientists maintain that rising temperatures could have far-reaching effects—some positive, some negative, and differing from region to region. But it is unlikely that the planetwide gloom and doom scenario depicted in movies such as *The Day After Tomorrow* will come to pass. Research on global warming should continue so that the world can better understand how accumulating greenhouse gases affect the present and the future. In doing so, people might stop fretting about the end of the world and instead work to build a better future.

Notes

1. Shaw, Jane S., ed. *Critical Thinking About Environmental Issues: Global Warming*. San Diego: Greenhaven, 2002.

2. Quoted in Shaw, ed. *Global Warming*.

3. Quoted in Shaw, ed. *Global Warming*.

4. Moore, Thomas Gale. "Happiness Is a Warm Planet." *Wall Street Journal* 7 Oct. 1997: 1.

Exercise A: Writing Introductions and Conclusions

Strong introductory and concluding paragraphs that quickly impart to your reader the essay's main idea can greatly enhance your essay. Well-written introductions not only present the essay's thesis statement, but also grab the attention of the reader and tell why the topic being explored is important and interesting. The conclusion reiterates the thesis statement, but also is the last chance for the writer to make an impression on the reader and to drive home his or her main points.

The Introduction

There are several techniques you can use in the opening paragraph to attract the reader's attention. An essay can start with

- an anecdote: a brief story that illustrates a point relevant to the topic;
- startling information: facts or statistics that clarify the point of the essay;
- setting up and knocking down a position: beginning the essay with an assertion proponents of one side of a controversy believe, and then raising questions about that assertion;
- summary information: general introductory information about the topic that feeds into the essay's thesis statement;
- historical perspective: an example of the way things used to be that leads into a discussion of how or why things work differently now.

Remember that in a cause-and-effect essay, the introductory paragraph should establish the cause that is being examined (for its multiple effects) or the effect that is being examined (for its multiple and/or chain-of-event causes).

1. Reread the introductory paragraphs of the model essays in this section and of the six viewpoints in the previous section. Identify which of the techniques described above are used in these essays. How else do they get the

attention of the reader while presenting the thesis statement of the essay?

2. Write an introduction for the essay you have outlined and partially written in the previous exercise. You can use one of the techniques described above.

The Conclusion

The conclusion brings the essay to a close by summarizing or restating its main argument(s). Good conclusions go beyond simply repeating the argument, however. They also answer the reader's question of "so what?" In other words, they tell why the argument is important to consider. Some conclusions may also explore the broader implications of the thesis argument. They may close with a quotation or refer back to an anecdote or event in the essay. In essays about controversial topics, such as global warming, the conclusion should reiterate what side the essay is taking.

3. Reread the concluding paragraphs of the model essays and of the six viewpoints of the previous section. Which were most effective in driving their arguments home to the reader? What sort of devices did they use?

4. Write a conclusion for the essay you have outlined and partially written in the previous exercise.

Author's Checklist

✔ Review the five-paragraph essay you've written.

✔ Make sure it has a clear introduction that draws the reader in and contains a thesis statement that concisely expresses what your essay is about.

✔ Evaluate the paragraphs and make sure they each have clear topic sentences that are well supported by interesting and relevant details.

✔ Check that you have used compelling and authoritative quotes to enliven the essay.

✔ Finally, be sure you have a solid conclusion that uses one of the techniques presented in this exercise.

Write Your Own Five-Paragraph Cause-and-Effect Essay

Using the material in this book, write your own five-paragraph cause-and-effect essay about global warming.

The following steps are suggestions on how to get started.

Step One: Choose your topic.

Think carefully before deciding on the topic of your essay. Is there any aspect of global warming that particularly fascinates you? Is there an issue you strongly support or feel strongly against? Ask yourself such questions before selecting your essay topic. Refer to Appendix C: Sample Essay Topics if you need help selecting a topic.

Step Two: Write down questions and answers about the topic.

Some possible questions to ask yourself might include

- Why is this topic important?
- Why should people be interested in this topic?
- What question am I going to answer in this paragraph or essay?
- How can I best answer this question?
- What facts or ideas can I use to support the answer to my question?
- How can I make this essay interesting to the reader?

Questions especially for cause-and-effect essays include

- What are the causes of the topic being examined?
- What are the effects of the topic being examined?
- Are there single or multiple causes?
- Are there single or multiple effects?
- Is a chain reaction of events involved?

Step Three: Gather facts and ideas related to your essay topic.

This volume contains several places to find information, including the viewpoints and the appendixes. In addition, you may want to research the books, articles, and Web sites listed in Section Three, or do additional research in your local library.

If you are using direct quotations or statements from someone, it is usually important to note their qualifications and possible biases.

Step Four: Develop a workable thesis statement.

Use what you have written down in steps two and three to help you choose the point you want to make in your essay.

Remember that the thesis statement has two parts: the topic (global warming) and the point of the essay. It should be expressed in a clear sentence and make an arguable or supportable point. In cause-and-effect essays, the thesis statement should include the cause and/or effect being examined.

Examples:

Global warming harms the environment.

This could be a multiple-effect essay that examines the effects of global warming on the environment.

Natural factors cause global warming.

This could be the basis for a multiple-cause essay on how sunspots, climatic cycles, and other natural factors (the causes) lead to global warming (the effect).

Step Five: Write an outline.

1. Write the thesis statement at the top.
2. Write roman numerals I, II, and III on the left side of the page with A, B, and C under each numeral.
3. Next to each roman numeral, write down the best arguments you came up with in step three. These should all directly relate to and support the thesis statement. If the essay is a multiple-cause essay, write down three causes; if it is a multiple-effect essay, write down three effects. If it is a chain of events, write down the events in sequence.

4. Next to each letter write down facts or information that supports that particular idea.

Step Six: Write the three supporting paragraphs.

Use your outline to write the three supporting paragraphs. Write down the main point of each paragraph in sentence form. Do the same for the supporting points of information. Each sentence should support the topic of the paragraph. Sometimes (not always), paragraphs include a concluding or summary sentence that restates the paragraph's argument.

Step Seven: Write the introduction and conclusion.

See Exercise A of Essay Three for information on writing introductions and conclusions.

Step Eight: Read and Rewrite

As you read, check your essay for the following:

- Does the essay maintain a consistent tone?

- Do all sentences serve to reinforce your general thesis or your paragraph topics?

- Do paragraphs flow from one to the other? Do you need to add transition words or phrases?

- Is there a sense of progression? Does each paragraph advance the argument by offering more information than preceding paragraphs?

- Does the essay get bogged down in too much detail or irrelevant material?

- Does your introduction grab the reader's attention?

- Does your conclusion give the essay a sense of closure?

- Are there any spelling or grammatical errors?

Tips on Writing Effective Cause-and-Effect Essays

✔ You do not need to describe every possible cause of an event or phenomenon. Focus on the most important ones that support your thesis statement.

✔ Vary your sentence structure; avoid repeating yourself.

✔ Maintain a professional, objective tone of voice. Avoid sounding uncertain or insulting.

✔ Anticipate what the reader's counterarguments may be and answer them.

✔ Use sources that state facts and other supporting evidence.

✔ Avoid assumptions or generalizations without evidence.

✔ Aim for clear, fluid, well-written sentences that together make up an essay that is informative, interesting, and memorable.

Section Three:
Supporting
Research
Material

Facts About Global Warming

Editor's Note: These facts can be used in reports or papers to reinforce or add credibility when making important points or claims.

Definitions and Origins of Global Warming

- Carbon dioxide, water vapor, nitrous oxide, and methane are known as *greenhouse gases*. In a process referred to as the *greenhouse effect*, these gases create a blanket of warm air around Earth. Without them, Earth would be an ice planet.
- The burning of fossil fuels (coal, oil, and natural gas) releases harmful pollutants as well as carbon dioxide, a greenhouse gas. This "extra" source of greenhouse gases in the atmosphere raises concerns about the effects of human-induced global warming.
- The phrase *global warming* most commonly refers to an increase in Earth's average temperature resulting from human activities.
- Humans began burning significant amounts of coal and other fossil fuels in the mid-1700s, at the beginning of the Industrial Revolution. Since then, atmospheric carbon dioxide levels have increased by nearly 30 percent.
- The global warming theory originated in 1896 when Swedish chemist Svante Arrhenius claimed that carbon dioxide emissions from the burning of fossil fuels would trap excess heat in Earth's atmosphere, thereby intensifying the greenhouse effect.
- The global warming hypothesis caught the world's attention in 1988 when James Hansen, an atmospheric scientist for NASA, testified before a U.S. Senate committee that rising temperatures would cause dramatic climate changes that could threaten environmental and human health.

- Fossil fuels account for 90 percent of the world's energy consumption.
- Over its lifetime the average car emits 50 tons of carbon dioxide into the atmosphere.
- Not all scientists believe that human activities are responsible for global warming. Sunspot activity and natural cyclic changes in Earth's climate also result in rising world temperatures.
- The current average worldwide temperature is 59°F (15°C).

Possible Negative Effects of Global Warming
- Earth has warmed about 1°F (0.556°C) over the past one hundred years.
- Global warming could lead to rising sea levels and changing rainfall amounts that could have negative effects on plants, wildlife, and humans.
- In the twentieth century the temperature increase In the Northern Hemisphere was greater than temperature increases for any other century in the last one thousand years.
- At the current rate of melting, all the glaciers in the U.S./Canadian Glacier National Park will be gone by 2070.
- The polar ice cap is melting at a rate of 9 percent per decade.
- Arctic ice thickness has decreased 40 percent since the 1960s.
- Over the past thirty years some Antarctic penguin populations have decreased by 33 percent as their sea-ice habitat disappears.
- Some climatologists predict that unless greenhouse gases are significantly reduced, U.S. temperatures will rise by 3° to 10°F (1.7° to 5.56°C) over the next one hundred years.
- Since 1980 Earth has experienced nineteen of its twenty hottest years on record, with 1998 being the hottest and 2002 and 2003 being the second and third hottest.

- Between 1970 and 1995 the Atlantic Ocean spawned an average of 4.9 hurricanes a year. After 1995 the average rose to 7.5 hurricanes a year. Since hurricanes develop over warm ocean waters, some scientists see a connection between global warming and increased hurricane activity.
- Global sea levels have risen between 4 and 8 inches (10 and 20cm) during the last one hundred years.
- Some scientists estimate that sea levels could rise an additional 19 to 37 inches (48 to 93cm) by the year 2100.
- More than 1 million species could become extinct by the year 2050 if greenhouse-gas pollution and global warming are not reduced.

Possible Benefits Related to Global Warming

- Measured temperature increases occur mostly at night and in the wintertime, which could lead to a decrease in cold-weather deaths and a longer growing season for crops.
- Warmer winters with less snow and ice would reduce accidents, transportation delays, and heating costs.
- Increased amounts of carbon dioxide in the air boost plants' ability to use water, enabling them to thrive with less water.
- Higher amounts of carbon dioxide enable many plants and crops to grow faster, bigger, and more profusely.
- Increased crop production would help to sustain a growing world population.
- More plentiful vegetation would absorb some carbon dioxide and prevent it from rising to dangerous levels in the atmosphere.

Finding and Using Sources of Information

No matter what type of essay you are writing, it is necessary to find information to support your point of view. You can use sources such as books, magazine articles, newspaper articles, and online articles.

Using Books and Articles

You can find books and articles in a library by using the library's computer or cataloging system. If you are not sure how to use these resources, ask a librarian to help you. You can also use a computer to find many magazine articles and other articles written specifically for the Internet.

You are likely to find a lot more information than you can possibly use in your essay, so your first task is to narrow it down to what is likely to be most usable. Look at book and article titles. Look at book chapter titles, and examine the book's index to see if it contains information on the specific topic you want to write about. (For example, if you want to write about alternative energy as a solution to global warming and you find a book about global warming, check the chapter titles and index to be sure it contains information about alternative energy before you check out the book.)

For a five-paragraph essay, you do not need a great deal of supporting information, so quickly try to narrow down your materials to a few good books and magazine or Internet articles. You do not need dozens. You might even find that one or two good books or articles contain all the information you need.

You probably do not have time to read an entire book, so find the chapters or sections that relate to your topic, and skim these. When you find useful information, copy it onto a notecard or into a notebook. You should look for supporting facts, statistics, quotations, and examples.

Using the Internet

When you select your supporting information, it is important that you evaluate its source. This is especially important with information you find on the Internet. Because nearly anyone can put information on the Internet, there is as much bad information as good information online. Before using Internet information—or any information— try to determine whether the source seems to be reliable. Is the author or Internet site sponsored by a legitimate organization? Is it from a government source? Does the author have any special knowledge or training relating to the topic you are looking up? Does the article give any indication of where its information comes from?

Using Your Supporting Information

When you use supporting information from a book, article, interview, or other source, there are three important things to remember:

1. *Make it clear whether you are using a direct quotation or a paraphrase.* If you copy information directly from your source, you are quoting it. You must put quotation marks around the information and tell where the information comes from. If you put the information in your own words, you are paraphrasing it.

Here is an example of a using a quotation:

According to the United Nations Framework Convention on Climate Change, "Most of the world's endangered species—some 25 percent of mammals and 12 percent of birds—may become extinct over the next few decades as warmer conditions alter the forests, wetlands, and rangelands they depend on."[1]

Here is an example of a brief paraphrase of the same passage:

According to the UN Framework Convention on Climate Change, global warming could cause the extinction of most of the planet's endangered species in the coming decades.

2. *Use the information fairly.* Be careful to use supporting information in the way the author intended it.

For example, it is unfair to quote an author as saying, "Global warming is a problem," when he or she actually said, "Global warming is a problem dreamed up by environmentalists." This is called taking information out of context. Using that information in such a way as supporting evidence is unfair.

3. *Give credit where credit is due.* Giving credit is known as citing. You must use citations when you use someone else's information, but not every piece of supporting information needs a citation.

- If the supporting information is general knowledge—that is, it can be found in many sources—you do not have to cite your source.
- If you directly quote a source, you must cite it.
- If you paraphrase information from a specific source, you must cite it.

If you do not use citations where you should, you are plagiarizing—or stealing—someone else's work.

Citing Your Sources

There are a number of ways to cite your sources. Your teacher will probably want you to do it in one of three ways:

- Informal: As in the examples in number 1 above, tell where you got the information in the same place you use it.
- Informal list: At the end of the article, place an unnumbered list of the sources you used. This tells the reader where, in general, you got your information.
- Formal: Use an endnote, as in the first example in number 1. (An endnote is generally placed at the end of an article or essay, although it may be located in different places depending on your teacher's requirements.)

Notes

1. United Nations Framework Convention on Climate Change. "Feeling the Heat." 24 Sept. 2005 < http://unfcc.int/2860.php > .

Using MLA Style to Create a Works Cited List

You will probably need to create a list of works cited for your paper. These include materials that you quoted from, relied heavily on, or consulted to write your paper. There are several different ways to structure these references. The following examples are based on Modern Language Association (MLA) style, one of the major citation styles used by writers.

Book Entries

For most book entries you will need the author's name, the book's title, where it was published, what company published it, and the year it was published. This information is usually found on the inside of the book. Variations on book entries include the following:

A book by a single author:
> Guest, Emma. *Children of AIDS: Africa's Orphan Crisis*. London: Sterling, 2003.

Two or more books by the same author:
> Friedman, Thomas L. *From Beirut to Jerusalem*. New York: Doubleday, 1989.
> ———. *The World Is Flat: A Brief History of the Twentieth Century*. New York: Farrar, Straus and Giroux, 2005.

A book by two or more authors:
> Pojman, Louis P., and Jeffrey Reiman. *The Death Penalty: For and Against*. Lanham, MD: Rowman & Littlefield, 1998.

A book with an editor:
> Friedman, Lauri S., ed. *At Issue: What Motivates Suicide Bombers?* San Diego, CA: Greenhaven, 2004.

Periodical and Newspaper Entries

Entries for sources found in periodicals and newspapers are cited a bit differently from books. For one, these sources usually have a title and a publication name. They also may have specific dates and page numbers. Unlike book entries, you do not need to list where newspapers or periodicals are published or what company publishes them.

An article from a periodical:
> Snow, Keith Harmon. "State Terror in Ethiopia." *Z Magazine* June 2004: 33–35.

An unsigned article from a periodical:
> "Broadcast Decency Rules." *Issues & Controversies on File* 30 Apr. 2004: 21–26.

An article from a newspaper:
> Constantino, Rebecca. "Fostering Love, Respecting Race." *Los Angeles Times* 14 Dec. 2002: B17.

Internet Sources

To document a source you found online, try to provide as much information on it as possible, including the author's name, the title of the document, the date of publication or of last revision, the URL, and your date of access.

A Web source:
> Shyovitz, David. "The History and Development of Yiddish." Jewish Virtual Library 30 May 2005 < http://www.jewishvirtuallibrary.org./jsource/History/yiddish.html > .

Your teacher will tell you exactly how information should be cited in your essay. Generally, the very least information needed is the original author's name and the name of the article or other publication.

Be sure you know exactly what information your teacher requires before you start looking for your supporting material so that you know what information to include with your notes.

Sample Essay Topics

The Theory of Global Warming Is Credible

The Theory of Global Warming Is Not Credible

Global Warming Is a Serious Problem

The Problem of Global Warming Has Been Exaggerated

Global Warming Will Have Detrimental Effects

Global Warming Will Have Beneficial Effects

Human Activity Contributes to Global Warming

Natural Factors Cause Global Warming

Alternative Energy Is a Solution to Global Warming

Alternative Energy Is Not a Solution to Global Warming

The United States Should Support the Kyoto Protocol

The United States Should Not Support the Kyoto Protocol

Organizations to Contact

Climate Solutions

219 Legion Way, Suite 201, Olympia, WA 98501-1113
(360) 352-1763 • fax: (360) 943-4977
e-mail: info@climatesolutions.org
Web site: http://climatesolutions.org

Climate Solutions' mission is to stop global warming at the earliest possible point by helping the northwest region of the United States develop practical and profitable solutions.

Competitive Enterprise Institute (CEI)

1001 Connecticut Ave. NW, Suite 1250, Washington, DC 20036
(202) 331-1010 • fax: (202) 331-0640
e-mail: info@cei.org • Web site: www.cei.org

CEI is a nonprofit organization dedicated to the principles of free enterprise and limited government. Rather than promoting government regulation, it advocates removing governmental barriers and using private incentives to protect the environment.

The George C. Marshall Institute

1625 K St. NW, Suite 1050, Washington, DC 20006
(202) 296-9655 • fax: (202) 296-9714
e-mail: info@marshall.org • Web site: www.marshall.org

The institute is a nonprofit research group that is dedicated to providing the public with clearly written and unbiased scientific and technical analyses of public policies. It publishes studies on global warming, including *Are Human Activities Causing Global Warming?*

Global Warming International Center (GWIC)

PO Box 50503, Palo Alto, CA 94303-0303
(630) 910-1551 • fax: (630) 910-1561
Web site: www.globalwarming.net

GWIC is an international body that disseminates information on global warming science and policy to governmental and nongovernmental organizations and industries in more than 120 countries.

The Heritage Foundation

214 Massachusetts Ave. NE, Washington, DC 20002-4999
(202) 546-4400 • fax: (202) 546-8328
e-mail: info@heritage.org • Web site: www.heritage.org

The Heritage Foundation is a think tank that supports free enterprise and limited government in environmental matters. Its publications include studies on the uncertainty of global warming and the greenhouse effect.

The Intergovernmental Panel on Climate Change (IPCC)

c/o World Meteorological Organization, 7bis Ave. de la Paix
C.P. 2300, Geneva 2, Switzerland CH-1211
+41-22-730-8208 • fax: +41-22-730-8025
e-mail: Ipcc-Sec@wmo.int • Web site: www.ipcc.ch

Established in 1988, the IPCC's role is to assess the scientific, social, and economic information relevant for the understanding of the risk of human-induced climate change.

Pew Center on Global Climate Change

2101 Wilson Blvd., Suite 550, Arlington, VA 22201
(703) 516-4146 • fax: (703) 841-1422
Web site: www.pewclimate.org

The Pew Center on Global Climate Change is a nonprofit and independent organization dedicated to educating the public and key policy makers about the causes and potential consequences of global climate change.

Sierra Club

85 2nd St., Second Fl., San Francisco, CA 94105
(415) 977-5500 • fax: (415) 977-5799

e-mail: information@sierraclub.org
Web site: www.sierraclub.org

The Sierra Club is a grassroots organization that promotes the protection and conservation of natural resources. It publishes the bimonthly magazine *Sierra* and special reports, including *Driving Up the Heat: SUVs and Global Warming*.

Union of Concerned Scientists (UCS)

2 Brattle Sq., Cambridge, MA 02238-9105
(617) 547-5552 • fax: (617) 864-9405
Web site: www.ucsusa.org

UCS works to advance responsible public policy in areas where science and technology play a vital role. Its programs focus on safe and renewable energy technologies, transportation reform, and sustainable agriculture.

Worldwatch Institute

1776 Massachusetts Ave. NW, Washington, DC 20036-1904
(202) 452-1999 • fax: (202) 296-7365
e-mail: worldwatch@worldwatch.org
Web site: www.worldwatch.org

The Worldwatch Institute is dedicated to fostering the evolution of a society in which human needs are met in ways that do not threaten the natural environment or the prospects of future generations. It publishes the annual *State of the World* anthology.

Bibliography

Books

Berger, John J., *Beating the Heat: Why and How We Must Combat Global Warming.* Berkeley, CA: Berkeley Hills, 2000.

Brown, Donald A., *American Heat.* Lanham, MD: Rowman & Littlefield, 2002.

Gelbspan, Ross, *Boiling Point: How Politicians, Big Oil and Coal, Journalists, and Activists Are Fueling the Climate Crisis— and What We Can Do to Avert Disaster.* New York: Basic Books, 2004.

Godrej, Dinyar, *The No-Nonsense Guide to Climate Change.* New York: Verso, 2001.

Green, Kenneth, *Global Warming: Understanding the Debate.* Berkeley Heights, NJ: Enslow, 2002.

Lim, Cheng Puay, *Our Warming Planet.* Chicago: Raintree, 2004.

Michaels, Patrick J., *Meltdown: The Predictable Distortion of Global Warming by Scientists, Politicians, and the Media.* Washington, DC: Cato Institute, 2004.

Silverstein, Alvin, et al., *Global Warming.* Brookfield, CT: Twenty-First Century, 2003.

Weart, Spencer, R., *The Discovery of Global Warming.* Cambridge, MA: Harvard University Press, 2003.

Periodicals

Anderson, Duncan Maxwell, "The Emperor's New Climate: Is Global Warming Real?" *Crisis,* February 2004.

Bethell, Tom, "The False Alert of Global Warming," *American Spectator,* May 2005.

Cheakalos, Christina, and Johnny Dodd, "Swallowed by the Sea: Threatened by Global Warming, Shishmaref's Eskimos Are Losing Their Island Home," *People,* February 24, 2003.

Eizenstat, Stuart E., and David B. Sandalow, "The Years After Tomorrow," *New York Times*, July 5, 2004.

Hayward, Steven F., "Cooled Down," *National Review*, January 31, 2005.

Kang, Hae Jin, "Hot and Bothered About Global Warming," *L.A. Youth*, March/April 2005.

Motavalli, Jim, "Too Darn Hot: Global Warming Accelerates the Spread of Disease," *E*, November/December 2004.

National Catholic Reporter, "Ignoring Evidence of Global Warming Is a Risky Gamble," January 11, 2002.

Perkins, Sid, "Dead Heat: The Health Consequences of Global Warming Could Be Many," *Science News*, July 3, 2004.

Petit, Charles W., "Arctic Thaw," *U.S. News & World Report*, November 8, 2004.

Reiter, Paul, "The Truth About Mosquitoes and Global Warming," *21st Century Science & Technology*, Winter 2003–2004.

Rohter, Larry, "Antarctica, Warming, Looks Ever More Vulnerable," *New York Times*, January 25, 2005.

Sawin, Janet L., "Global Warming's Impacts Evident Worldwide," *World Watch*, March/April 2005.

Schueller, Gretel H., "For the Earth, the Heat Is On," *Popular Science*, January 1, 2005.

Turner, Kelly, "Playing It Cool: Stop the Finger Pointing and Start the Problem Solving. Here's What You, and the Government, Can Do to Stop Global Warming," *Audubon*, December 2003.

Wall Street Journal, "Kyoto by Degrees," June 21, 2005.

Wohlforth, Charles, "A Romance with Oil in a Melting World," *Los Angeles Times*, June 14, 2004.

Index

Picture Credits

About the Editor

Mary E. Williams earned a master's in fine arts degree from San Diego State University, where she studied comparative literature, poetry, and creative writing. Williams has an enduring interest in race relations, world religions, and social justice. An editor for Greenhaven Press since 1996, she lives in San Marcos, California, with her husband, Kirk Takvorian.